THE 3-D PAPER BOOK

BY HANNAH TOFTS

Written and Edited by Diane James
Photography by Jon Barnes

CONTENTS

SIMON AND SCHUSTER BOOKS FOR YOUNG READERS

Simon & Schuster Building, Rockefeller Center, 1230 Avenue of the Americas, New York, New York 10020
Text and compilation copyright © 1989 by Two-Can Publishing Ltd. Illustration and design copyright © 1989 by Hannah Tofts. All rights reserved including the right of reproduction in whole or in part in any form. Originally published in Great Britain by Two-Can Publishing Ltd. First U.S. edition 1990. SIMON AND SCHUSTER BOOKS FOR YOUNG READERS is a trademark of Simon & Schuster Inc. Manufactured in Portugal.

10 9 8 7 6 5 4 3 2 1   (pbk.) 10 9 8 7 6 5 4 3 2 1

Library of Congress Cataloging-in-Publication Data: Tofts, Hannah. The 3-D paper book / by Hannah Tofts ; edited by Diane James ; photography by Jon Barnes.— 1st U.S. ed.   Summary: Provides illustrated instructions for a variety of paper modelling activities. 1. Paper work—Juvenile literature. 2. Models and modelmaking—Juvenile literature. [1. Paper work. 2. Models and modelmaking.] I. James, Diane. II. Barnes, Jon, ill. III. Title. IV. Title: Three-D paper book. TT870.T64 1990 745.54—dc20 89-27416 CIP AC

ISBN 0-671-70370-6   ISBN 0-671-70371-4 (pbk.)

EQUIPMENT

In this book you will find lots of different ways to give shape to flat paper and cardboard. Make a collection of empty cardboard packets and boxes, cardboard tubes, and old egg cartons. Look for cardboard that has an interesting texture, such as the corrugated kind. Gather together the basic equipment shown on these pages for cutting, gluing, and painting. Have fun experimenting!

cardboard cartons

craft knife

cardboard tubes

collection of cardboard and paper

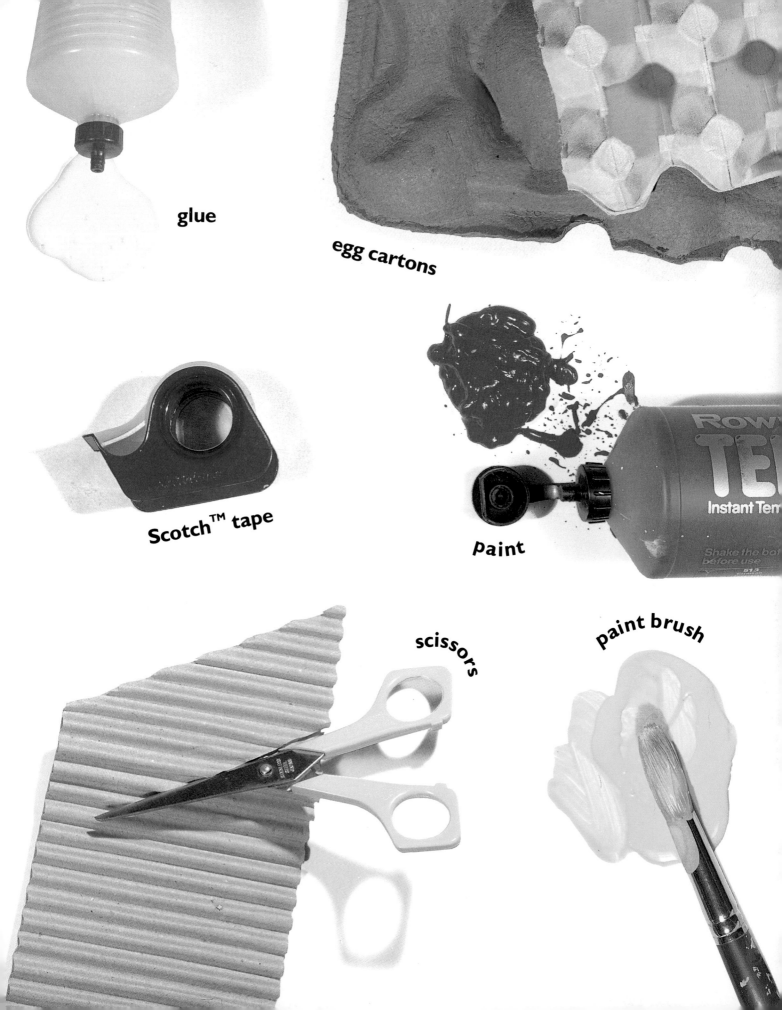

glue

egg cartons

Scotch™ tape

paint

scissors

paint brush

Here are some suggestions for altering the shape of a flat piece of paper using simple cuts. Try cutting half squares, circles, and triangles like the ones at the top of the picture. Fold back every other strip of paper.

To make the wavy triangles, first score the wavy lines on the paper. Cut triangles – as in the picture below – from one score line to the other. Fold the triangles upwards. Try scoring and cutting other simple shapes.

Try cutting wide strips out of the paper and rolling the ends around a fat pencil to make paper rolls.

Here are some more ideas for cutting and scoring using accordion folds. Score straight lines down a sheet of paper or thin cardboard using a ruler and a scoring tool. Make accordion folds along the score lines.

Use a pencil and ruler to draw squares or triangles in the center of a fold. The picture below shows how to do this. Score along the dotted lines with a craft knife. Gently push the shapes up or down, away from the fold.

This picture was made simply by gluing cardboard shapes on top of each other. First sketch out a rough design and work out how your layers will build up. Cut shapes from thick, soft cardboard and paint them. Glue the shapes in position. Watch how the shapes begin to make shadows as they build up.

To make a 3-D picture like this one, you will need a good collection of interesting shapes. Look for lots of different boxes, tubes, cartons, and packaging materials. Lay your collection out and play around with the shapes until you have a well-balanced pattern. Either paint the shapes before you glue them down or use spray paint afterwards.

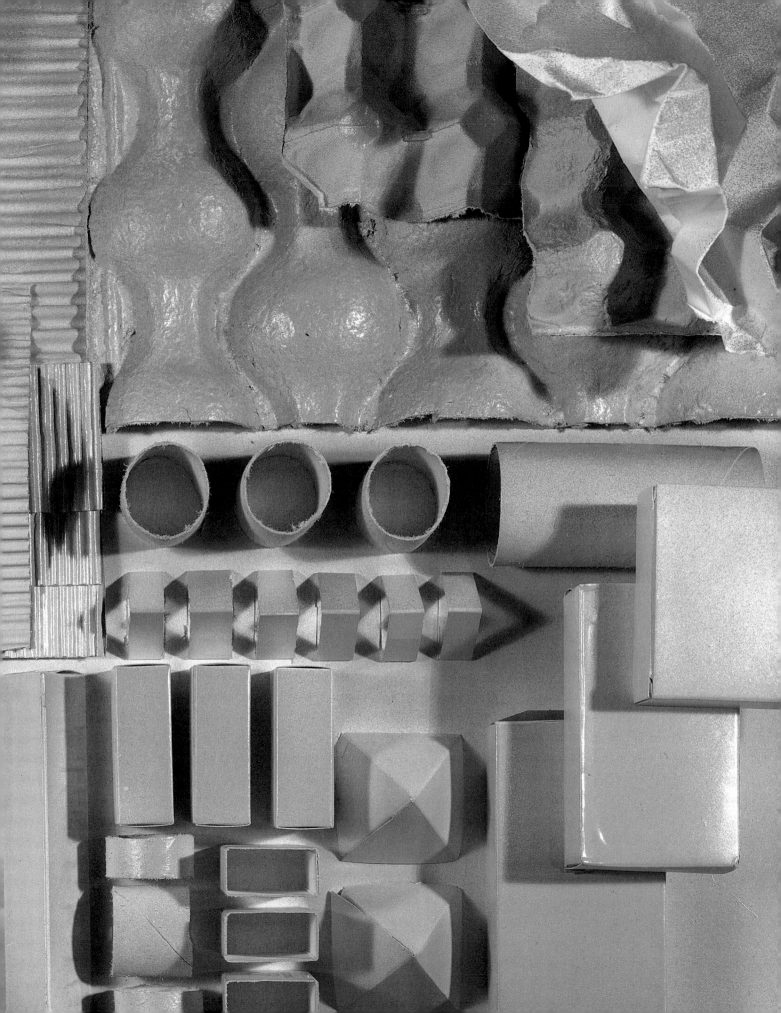

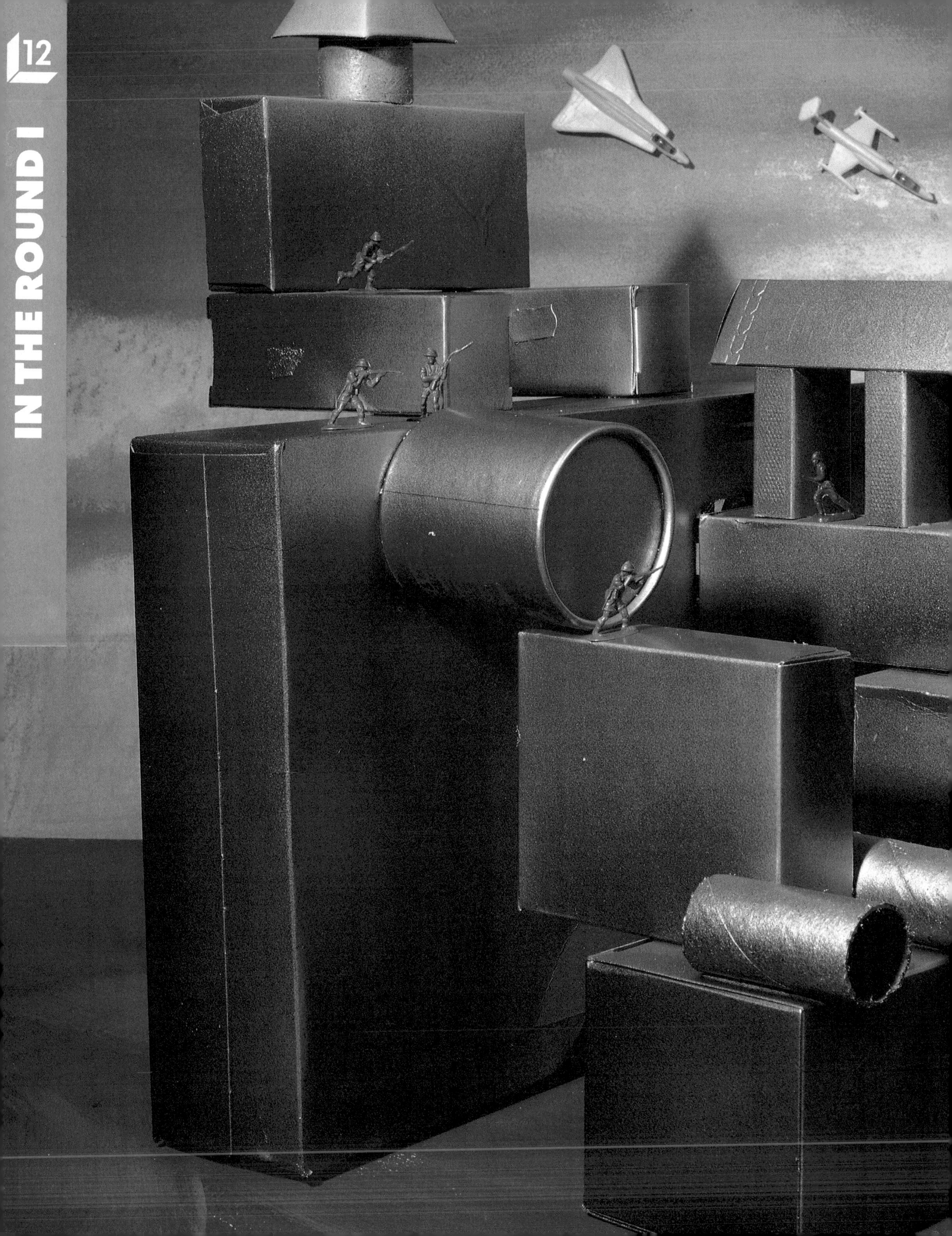

Next time you are in a city, look at the shapes of the buildings. Can you see any round towers, large pillars, giant domes, or tall steeples? Make a collection of cardboard boxes, tubes, and cartons. Try constructing your own building using this collection. Stick the pieces together with strong glue.

Invite your friends to a party and surprise them with this wonderful spread of cardboard food! Using the methods from the rest of this book, see how many different kinds of cookies and cakes you can make. Decorate your food with paper curls, flags, and shapes made from corrugated cardboard, or pleated paper.

Fold a sheet of cardboard or stiff paper in half. Draw a shape on the cardboard and cut around it. Do not cut along the fold or your shape will not stand up!

The dog's head was cut out separately, allowing for a tab on the end. The tab was then slotted through a slit made in the body. The pineapple leaves were done in the same way.

When slotting shapes together, make sure that the slit is exactly the same length as the tab that will be slotted through. Glue or tape the tab in position on the inside.

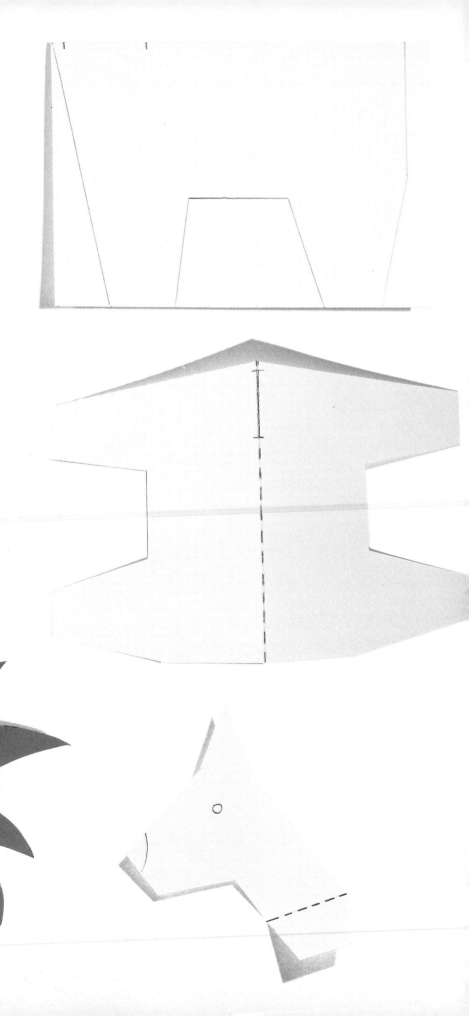

By using paper fasteners, which you can buy in stationery and craft stores, you can make models that move!

Try to find fairly thick but soft cardboard, such as old fruit boxes.

First, decide on the shape of your model and which pieces you want to move.

On our alligator, the jaws will open and shut and the legs will move. The bird's wings move up and down.

Make a sketch of your model and then cut the pieces out of cardboard. Pierce holes through the parts where the "joint" will be and push a paper fastener through. Flatten out the ends of the paper fastener so that it doesn't fall out. It is easier to paint the pieces of your model before you put the paper fasteners in.

By making simple slits in pieces of cardboard, you can make almost any shape stand on its own!

Make wide slits by cutting twice, so that the pieces slot together neatly. On one cardboard shape the slit should start at the top. On the other it should start at the bottom. Slits should usually be slightly more than half the height of the shape. The pictures on this page show different methods for slitting and slotting cardboard shapes together.

You can also make a flat piece of cardboard stand up by folding it along the middle.

Some pop-ups are made by cutting and scoring. Others are made by gluing on extra bits of paper. To make the dancing girl, first mark the center of a sheet of cardboard or stiff paper. Cut out a blouse shape and glue it down the center fold.

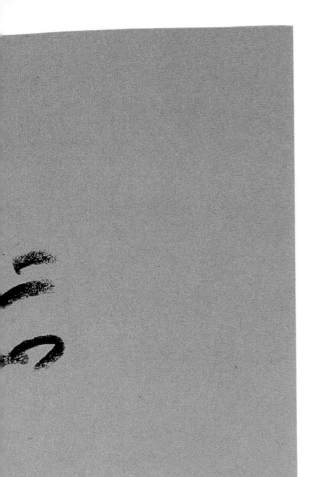

This Christmas tree card was made by cutting and scoring. Cut out a rectangle of white cardboard and mark the center line. Glue a green triangle for the tree and a red rectangle for the container. Fold the card in half. Cut along the bottom of the tree and the top and bottom of the container. Score down the sides of the tree and container to make them pop up!

Make the skirt by pleating a length of colored paper. Glue down the edges of the skirt at an angle to the center fold. Carefully close the card. When you open the card, the skirt will pop out! Now try experimenting with your own ideas.

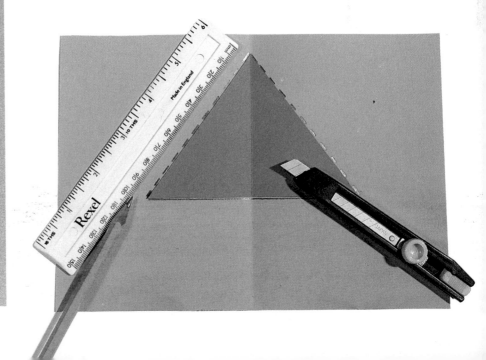

These pop-up cards are made by cutting and scoring. The main shapes stay attached to the card by tabs. First, mark the center of a piece of cardboard. Draw the main part of your picture on the lower half of the card. Decide where the tabs should go. (If it is a large drawing, you will need two tabs.) Draw in the tabs. The length of the tabs should be equal to the distance from the bottom of your drawing to the center fold. Look at the picture opposite: the blue lines show score lines and the pencil lines show cutting lines. Cut and score the picture and the tabs, and push them out from the background.

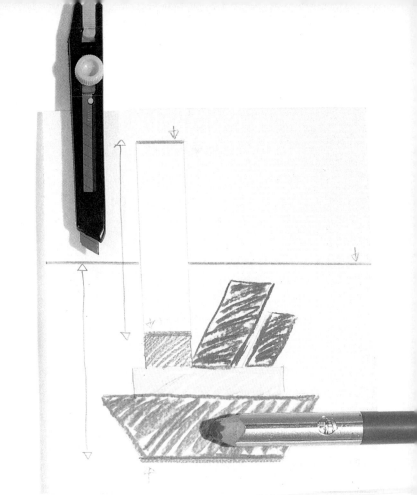

To make moving parts, fold under one edge of the card and tape it down to make a pocket. Cut a window in the front of the pocket and put a strip of cardboard slightly longer than the pocket inside. Pull the strip in and out!

Create your own theater, actors, and scenery from a shoe box and some pieces of cardboard! Invite your friends over and perform your favorite plays with your own characters. On the next two pages you will find out how we made our theater by slotting in some of the scenery from the top and moving other pieces backwards and forwards from the sides.

Use a shoe box or a fruit box to make the frame for your theater. Cut out a rectangle at one of the short ends, leaving a narrow frame. Make a decorated front from a piece of thin cardboard and glue it to the frame.

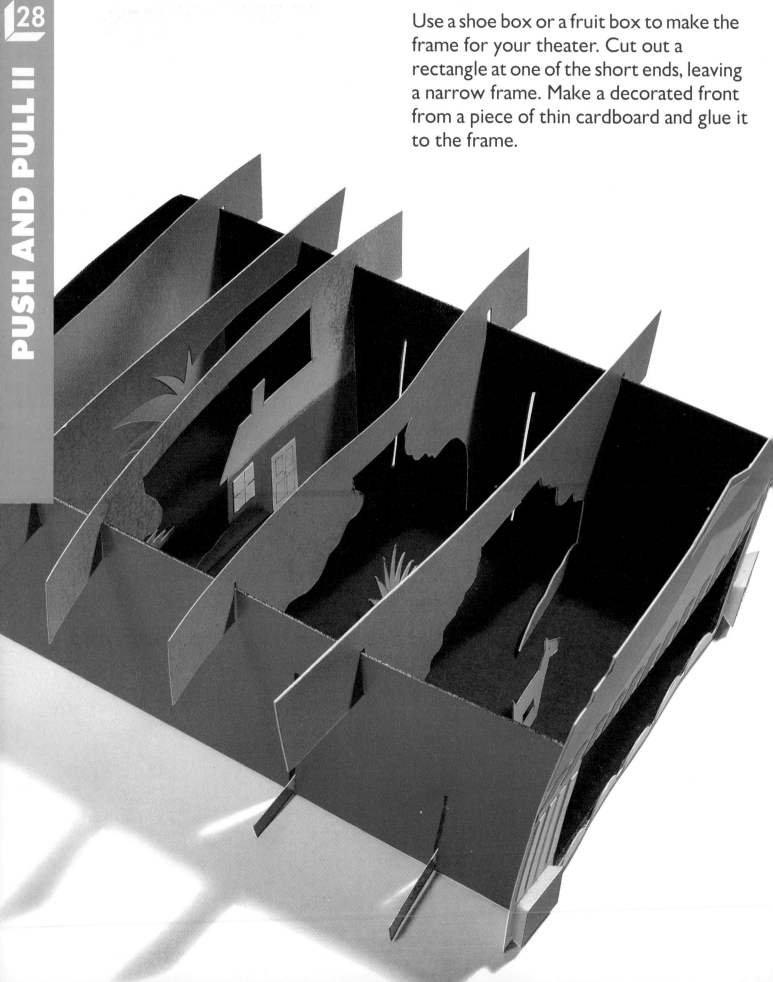

Make a selection of backdrops from pieces of thin cardboard. The backdrops should be slightly higher than the shoe box. Cut slits about 3 knife cuts wide, so that the backdrops slot comfortably over the sides of the box. The distance from the top of the slot to the bottom of the backdrop should be the same height as the box. You can make curtains for your theater in the same way.

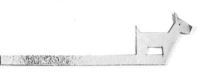

To make characters and props, draw and cut out the shapes, leaving a length of thin cardboard attached. Make slits in the sides of the box high enough to push the characters through.

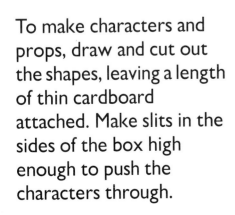

Here are some delicious fruits and vegetables – but they are not for eating! All the examples here are made from papier-mâché – a mixture of paste and paper. On the next page you will find the paste recipe and tips for making the basic framework for objects.

Paste Recipe

1. Measure out a cup of flour and 3 cups of water.

2. In a saucepan, mix a little of the water with the flour to make a smooth paste.

3. Add the rest of the water and ask a grown-up to heat the mixture until it boils – they must keep stirring all the time! Turn the heat down and let the mixture simmer until the paste thickens.

4. Leave the mixture until it is cold.

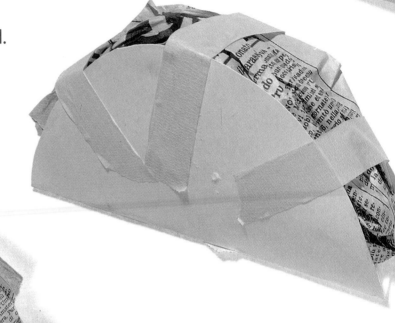

Decide what shape you want your finished object to be. Make a framework from cardboard and newspaper, using tape to keep it in position. Paste on layers of newspaper, molding the layers as you go along to make a good shape. Leave your object to dry and then paint and varnish it.